For Zuey, Leykh, and Arjun,
and for you—diamonds who shine

First edition 2024

Library of Congress Catalog Card Number 2023943604
ISBN 978-1-5362-2829-8

APS 29 28 27 26 25 24
10 9 8 7 6 5 4 3 2 1

Printed in Humen, Dongguan, China

This book was typeset in Papercuts, Chelsea Market,
and Kohinoor, a humanist sans serif font designed
by Satya Rajpurohit for the Indian Type Foundry.
The illustrations were collaged, by hand and
digitally, with cut paper and other materials.

Candlewick Press
99 Dover Street
Somerville, Massachusetts 02144

www.candlewick.com

AND YET YOU SHINE

The Kohinoor Diamond, Colonization, and Resistance

Supriya Kelkar

CANDLEWICK PRESS

Washed away by rippling waves,
you sink in sandy sediment,
caressed by your land . . .

until a pair of brown hands
sifts through the grains
and you emerge.

Look at your shine!

You find your place
in the Peacock Throne,
seven long years in the making—
a sight to see,
a jewel among gems.

And, oh, how you shine.

But soon, all around you,
the soil turns crimson
and cries fill the air.

So much gold,
so many gemstones—
stolen.

Seven hundred camels
4,000 elephants
12,000 horses
are needed
just to haul
the loot away.

You're ripped from your throne,
placed on an arm,
pulled away from your home.

And yet you shine.

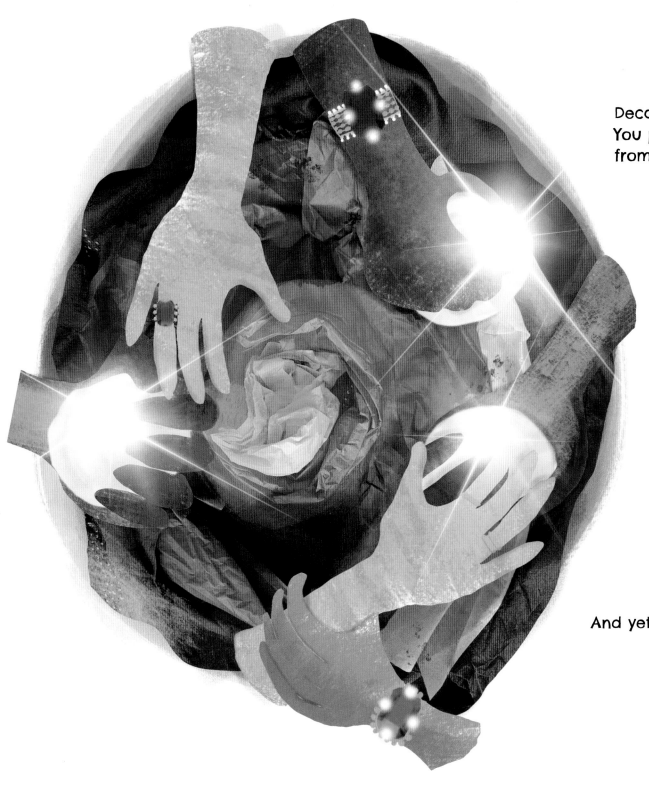

Decades pass.
You pass
from hand to hand.

One unspeakable act
after another
just to rule over you.

And yet you shine.

Finally, you're back home—
the land where those brown hands
first unearthed you.

But it isn't the home you left.

People have come.
People who want to take
what your land grows.

People who want to own
what those in your land make.

People who want to hurt others—
if it helps them,
if it makes them rich—
no matter the cost.

And they have their eyes
on
you.

For the time being
you are safe.
You're with the next in line for the crown:

a boy
just ten years old.

Scared and alone,
forcibly separated from his mother,
trying to do what's right.

But the colonizers
trick the boy,
make him sign you away.

Once more, you're stolen.
Taken from your home yet again.
Traveling by waves—
not to your birthplace like before.

No.
You are off to become a symbol
of the power of your colonizers.
A treasure to be shown off.
A trophy for the Queen of England.
A prized part of a collection of conquests.

And yet you shine.

Just not enough for their standards.

You're chopped at—
recut
reshaped
polished to look brand new.

They've brought you down.
You're half your original size now.

Again you are on display—now the crown jewel
for all to see,
for all to know
you are theirs.

They have won.
They are in charge.
They are unstoppable—

DO NOT TOUCH

and
yet
you
shine.

Why do you shine, though?
After everything you've been through—
after being told you're not good enough for their standards,
after being told you should look different to belong,
after being cut down, torn down,
like a piece of property just passing hands?

It's because you know you are a diamond.

A dazzling, brilliant diamond.

And no matter what,
they can't
they won't
they'll never dull

your shine.

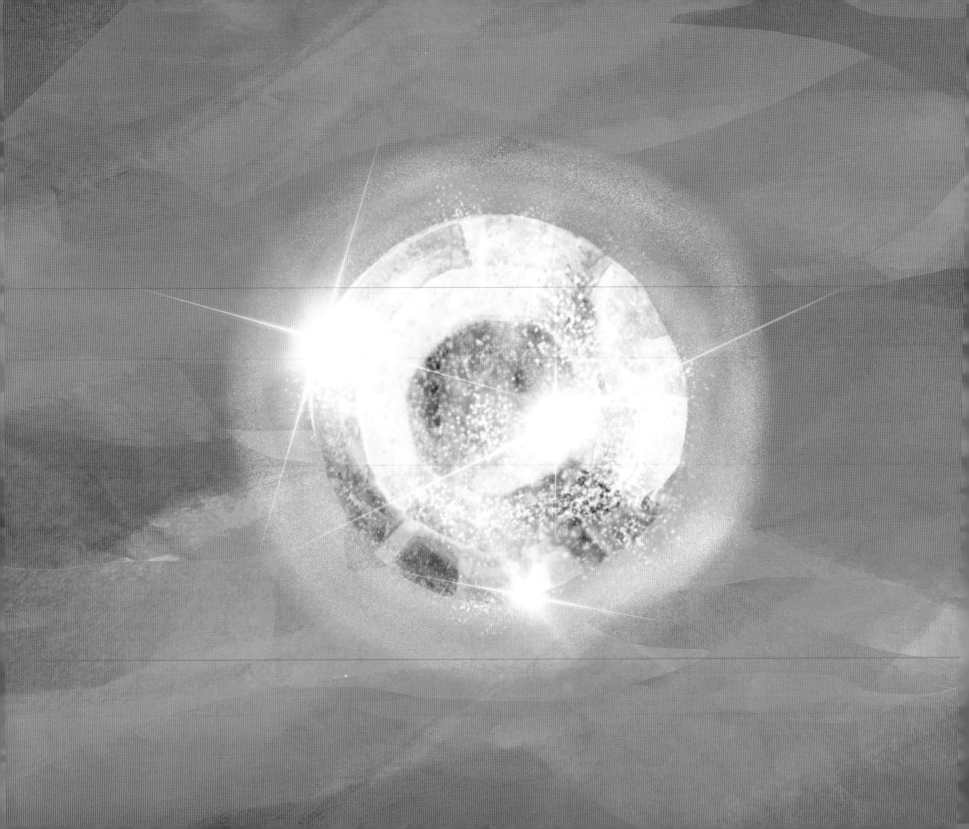

THE KOHINOOR DIAMOND
A HISTORY OF LOOTING AND THEFT

The massive Kohinoor (also spelled *Koh-i-Noor*) diamond is first mentioned in historical records about the Mughal Dynasty, which was founded in 1526 by Zahiruddin Babur after he invaded South Asia from Central Asia. In 1628, Mughal emperor Shah Jahan (who would go on to commission the building of the Taj Mahal) ordered a magnificent throne encrusted with colorful gemstones, some of which formed the shape of peacocks. The Kohinoor diamond was set in the head of one of these jeweled peacocks.

A century later, ruler Nadir Shah (also spelled *Nader Shah*), creator of a sprawling Iranian empire, invaded Delhi and looted so many gemstones and so much gold that it took hundreds of elephants and thousands of horses and camels to haul it all away. The peacock throne was among his plunder. He removed the Kohinoor diamond from it and had it fashioned into an armlet.

For decades, the Kohinoor diamond passed from ruler to ruler amid terrible acts of violence until it finally returned to India.

But the India it returned to had changed. Much of it had been taken over by the British East India Company, colonizers from England whose sole purpose was to loot South Asia, strip it of its resources and of the products its people were famous for making, and get rich—no matter the cost of lives and livelihoods among South Asians.

By this time, the Kohinoor diamond was famous for being so big and had become a symbol of power. The British wanted the diamond to further prove their power to the world.

But the Kohinoor diamond was in the possession of Ranjit Singh, maharaja of the Sikh Empire, who had taken it from Shah Shuja Durrani, ruler of the Durrani Empire. On his deathbed, Maharaja Ranjit Singh began to give away several of his prized possessions to religious institutions of various faiths. Maharaja Ranjit Singh died in 1839, and some thought that he had planned to will the diamond to Hindu priests.

Many people in England were furious that such a famous, large, expensive diamond might go to Hindu priests. They wanted the diamond in British hands.

After Maharaja Ranjit Singh's death, the diamond passed hands through assassinations and turmoil until it ended up belonging to Maharani Jindan Kaur and her five-year-old son and heir to the throne, Duleep Singh, who wore the diamond on his upper arm.

In 1849, after the British empire violently expanded their dominion, they imprisoned the maharani and forced the now ten-year-old boy-king to sign over his kingdom—and the Kohinoor diamond. Duleep Singh was kept as a prized ward of the British and wasn't allowed to be reunited with his mother until years later, in 1861, when he was a grown man.

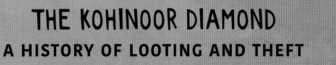

Meanwhile, the Kohinoor diamond was taken to England, where it served as a trophy for Queen Victoria, to show off the British conquest of South Asia: a symbol of victory and power.

Despite all of the hoopla surrounding the diamond, when it was publicly displayed at the Great Exhibition in 1851, many visitors found it less dazzling than they had expected. Their disappointment upset Queen Victoria's husband, Prince Albert, who demanded that the diamond be recut and reshaped to fit Western standards of beauty. The diamond was chopped down to half its size in the process of becoming shinier for the colonizing prince and queen of England.

The recut diamond was made into a brooch that Queen Victoria proudly wore. It then became a part of the crown jewels and was worn by several queens down the line, including the Queen Mother, Queen Elizabeth II's mother. The crown rested atop her coffin during her funeral.

At one point, several articles speculated that Camilla, the new queen consort, might be wearing the Kohinoor or a replica of it in a crown at Charles's coronation, until activism and media attention called out the fact that the Kohinoor was one of the many stolen diamonds in the crown jewels.

The Kohinoor diamond still sits in England, in the Jewel House at the Tower of London, on display along with many other stolen artifacts from South Asia and elsewhere, places the British East India Company, Crown, and government devastatingly colonized.

ALLUVIAL MINING

Alluvial mining was the way diamonds were mined in ancient India. When mineral deposits erode and are washed to a new location by a body of water, the sediments are deposited. They can then be sifted by hand by alluvial miners. The Kohinoor diamond was found through alluvial mining, which is also how many people in the United States looked for gold during the Gold Rush.

WHAT IS COLONIZATION?

Colonization is the act of taking control over a land and its people. Many European powers—including the Dutch, French, Portuguese, and British—invaded India to colonize its inhabitants and land, at a terrible cost to the Indigenous populations.

It was said that at its height, the sun never set on the vastness of the British empire. Because the British empire was based on the brutal colonization of people and places all around the world, when it was daytime on one side of their territory, it was night on the other, and vice versa, so the sun was always shining down on their massive stolen lands.

In South Asia, the British colonizers diverted native-grown grains to England, leaving millions of South Asians to die during famines. They also imposed a devious system of taxation, taxing artisans for creating goods that were prized around the world, then using a portion of the money they collected to purchase the artisans' goods, basically getting the goods for free. Indians were also coerced into indentured servitude and taken to the Caribbean and Africa to work on British plantations under harsh conditions.

The English word *loot* comes from India via colonization, from the Hindi word *lut*. Some economists think that in today's money, the British colonial regime looted 45 trillion dollars from South Asia. The money helped advance Europe and contributed to the Industrial Revolution—at a great cost to South Asians.

The effects of colonization can still be seen today, as many of the poorest nations in the world are lands that were stripped of their resources by colonizers.

HOW CAN YOU DECOLONIZE?

Decolonization—the act of removing the toxic influence of colonizers—is not just a matter of removing a group of people from a place they have colonized. It is also a matter of unlearning and rejecting the mindsets that colonizers imposed.

Here are just some of the many ways we can unlearn some of the things colonization has enforced within us:

- Expanding beauty standards: Ideas about beauty often center one type of look over others. Knowing that we come in all different shapes and sizes, with different-shaped facial features and different textures of hair, and recognizing *all* of them as valid and important, can help undo some of the damage colonization has done in holding one look higher than others.

- Pronouncing your name and others' names correctly: Mispronouncing your name to make it easier for someone else to pronounce is a form of colonization. And pronouncing someone else's name incorrectly—or *changing* someone else's name because you find their real name hard to pronounce—is a form of colonization. Making sure you pronounce your name the way it is meant to be said, the way you want it to be said, is an important way to honor the history that comes with that name, as is taking the time to learn how to pronounce other people's names correctly.

- Acknowledging injustices: Past injustices are often swept under the rug because it makes the people in power uncomfortable to acknowledge their (or their predecessors') wrongdoings. By becoming aware of past injustices, by understanding how they shape the world we live in now—how they are ingrained within the power dynamics, resources, and financial state of countries, including our own—we can start to challenge the myths that colonization has told us.

- Questioning whose story is being told and who is telling it: Thinking about whose story is erased—in social studies, history, and books—and whose story is being centered is an important part of decolonization. Colonizers are often portrayed as brave explorers who "discovered new lands" and helped the Indigenous peoples in those lands by introducing

their way of life to them and imposing their beliefs and values on them to "make them better." But this story of colonizers as heroes is far from the truth. In reality, colonization is a brutal, devastating, racist, and cruel practice that has wreaked havoc on people around the world, leading to the erosion or erasure of their cultures, languages, religions, and identities, and often costing them their lives or their livelihoods.

A FEW FACTS

- Except for some black diamonds found in Borneo, India was the only source of diamonds until 1725, when diamond deposits were discovered in Brazil.

- The world's oldest texts on gemology come from India.

- The original, egg-shaped Kohinoor diamond weighed 190.3 carats before it was recut and reduced to 93 carats.

- The Kohinoor diamond is now the ninetieth-largest diamond in the world.

- In the past, South Asia consisted of several kingdoms and Indigenous lands before it became the countries that make up the region today. The area was called by many different names depending on who was referring to it and during what period. British India consisted of regions in the present-day countries of India, Pakistan, Bangladesh, and Myanmar. Other South Asian countries were also controlled by the British in part but not considered part of British India.

WHAT SHOULD HAPPEN TO STOLEN TREASURES AND ARTIFACTS IN MUSEUMS?

Just like the Kohinoor diamond, many artworks and artifacts in museums around the world were procured through colonial theft. What should happen to these stolen objects?

There is a movement to return the pieces to their rightful owners. In many cases, however, it is hard to determine the rightful owners because there are conflicting claims to the ownership of the artifact or because colonization led to the creation of new countries out of kingdoms and lands with their own histories.

Some people argue that the artifacts are safest in museums that house stolen goods because that way, their location is widely known and they can be preserved and displayed for everyone to study. But this line of thinking assumes that the artifacts are safer in the hands of colonizers and that the Indigenous peoples from whom they were taken can't be trusted with them.

What do *you* think should happen to the looted artifacts?

FOR FURTHER EXPLORATION

Daniels, Nicole. "Should Museums Return Looted Artifacts to Their Countries of Origin?" Student Opinion, *New York Times*, October 16, 2020. https://www.nytimes.com/2020 /10/16/learning/should-museums-return-looted-artifacts-to-their-countries-of-origin.html.

"Koh-i-Noor: Six Myths about a Priceless Diamond." BBC News, December 9, 2016. https://www.bbc.com/news/world-asia-india-38218308.

BIBLIOGRAPHY

Alberge, Dalya. "British Museum Is World's Largest Receiver of Stolen Goods, Says QC." *Guardian*, November 4, 2019. https://www.theguardian.com/world/2019/nov/04 /british-museum-is-worlds-largest-receiver-of-stolen-goods-says-qc.

Boissoneault, Lorraine. "The True Story of the Koh-i-Noor Diamond—and Why the British Won't Give It Back." *Smithsonian*, August 30, 2017. https://www.smithsonianmag.com/history /true-story-koh-i-noor-diamondand-why-british-wont-give-it-back-180964660/.

Chaudhury, Dipanjan Roy. "British Looted $45 Trillion from India in Today's Value: Jaishankar." *Economic Times*, updated October 3, 2019. https://economictimes.indiatimes.com/news /politics-and-nation/british-looted-45-trillion-from-india-in-todays-valuejaishankar /articleshow/71426353.cms?from=mdr.

Dalrymple, William, and Anita Anand. *Koh-i-noor: The History of the World's Most Infamous Diamond*. New York: Bloomsbury, 2017.

"Desired, Stolen, Cursed: The History of the Koh-i-Noor Diamond." History Extra, February 4, 2020. https://www.historyextra.com/period/victorian/koh-i-noor-diamond-what-happened-who-owns/.

"India: Map of British India and Adjacent Countries." New York State Archives, NYSA_ A3045-78_3178. https://digitalcollections.archives.nysed.gov/index.php.

Kaur, Brahmjot. "Camilla Swaps the Kohinoor Diamond for Another Controversial Stone on Her Coronation Crown." *NBC News*, February 17, 2023. https://www.nbcnews.com/news/asian-america /camilla-swaps-kohinoor-diamond-another-controversial-stone-coronation-rcna71032.

Pistilli, Melissa. "Alluvial Mining: Gold, Diamonds and Platinum." INN (Investing News Network), March 17, 2022. https://investingnews.com/daily/resource-investing/precious-metals-investing /gold-investing/alluvial-mining-gold-diamonds-and-platinum/.

Robertson, Geoffrey. "It's Time for Museums to Return Their Stolen Treasures." CNN Style, updated June 11, 2020. https://www.cnn.com/style/article/return-stolen-treasures-geoffrey-robertson /index.html.